A Note From Rick Renner

I am on a personal quest to see a "revival of
the Bible" so people can establish their lives on
a firm foundation that will stand strong and
endure the test as end-time storm winds begin
to intensify.

In order to experience a revival of the Bible in
your personal life, it is important to take time
each day to read, receive, and apply its truths to your life. James tells us
that if we will continue in the perfect law of liberty — refusing to be
forgetful hearers, but determined to be doers — we will be blessed in
our ways. As you watch or listen to the programs in this series and work
through this corresponding study guide, I trust you will search the Scriptures and allow the Holy Spirit to help you hear something new from
God's Word that applies specifically to your life. I encourage you to be a
doer of the Word He reveals to you. Whatever the cost, I assure you — it
will be worth it.

> Thy words were found, and I did eat them;
> and thy word was unto me the joy and rejoicing of mine heart:
> for I am called by thy name, O Lord God of hosts.
> — Jeremiah 15:16

Your brother and friend in Jesus Christ,

Rick Renner

You Are God's Restoration Project
How God Restores the Desolate Places in Your Life

Published by Rick Renner Ministries
www.renner.org

ISBN 13: 978-1-6675-0027-0

eBook ISBN 13: 978-1-6675-0028-7

How To Use This Study Guide

This five-lesson study guide corresponds to *"You Are God's Restoration Project" With Rick Renner* (Renner TV). Each lesson in this study guide covers a topic that is addressed during the program series, with questions and references supplied to draw you deeper into your own private study of the Scriptures on this subject.

To derive the most benefit from this study guide, consider the following:

First, watch or listen to the program prior to working through the corresponding lesson in this guide. (Programs can also be viewed at **renner.org** by clicking on the Media/Archives links or on our Renner Ministries YouTube channel.)

Second, take the time to look up the scriptures included in each lesson. Prayerfully consider their application to your own life.

Third, use a journal or notebook to make note of your answers to each lesson's Study Questions and Practical Application challenges.

Fourth, invest specific time in prayer and in the Word of God to consult with the Holy Spirit. Write down the scriptures or insights He reveals to you.

Finally, take action! Whatever the Lord tells you to do according to His Word, do it.

For added insights on this subject, it is recommended that you obtain Denise Renner's book bundle, which includes *Who Stole Cinderella? — The Art of Happily Ever After, The Gift of Forgiveness, Do You Know What Time It Is?,* and *Redeemed From Shame.* You may also select from Rick Renner's available resources by placing your order at **renner.org** or by calling 1-800-742-5593.

TOPIC

Jesus Can Restore Whatever the Devil Has Tried To Steal, Kill, and Destroy in Your Life

SCRIPTURES

1. **John 10:10** — The thief cometh not, but for to steal, and to kill, and to destroy: I am come that they might have life, and that they might have it more abundantly.

2. **Luke 3:16** — ...But one mightier than I cometh, the latchet of whose shoes I am not worthy to unloose....

GREEK WORDS

1. "thief" — **κλέπτης** (*kleptes*): a bandit, thief, or scam artist

2. "steal" — **κλέπτω** (*klepto*): one so artful in the way he steals that his exploits of thievery are nearly undetectable; a pickpocket; it is where we get the word kleptomaniac

3. "kill" — **θύω** (*thuo*): not kill, as in murder, but to sacrifice; a religious sacrifice; to surrender or to give up something that is precious and dear

4. "destroy" — **ἀπόλλυμι** (*apollumi*): to ruin, waste, trash, devastate, or destroy

5. "life" — **ζωή** (*zoe*): life filled with vitality

6. "abundantly" — **περισσός** (*perissos*): abundantly; excessively; exceedingly; extraordinary; something that abounds in an extraordinary measure; so profuse that it can be likened to a river overflowing and flooding beyond its banks; overflowing, plentiful, or even superabundant

SYNOPSIS

The five lessons in this study on *You Are God's Restoration Project* will focus on the following topics:

- Jesus Can Restore Whatever the Devil Has Tried To Steal, Kill, and Destroy in Your Life
- Jesus Can Restore You From Any Abuse You Have Experienced
- Jesus Can Masterfully Restore You
- Jesus Is in the Restoration Business
- Jesus Can Restore the Years You Have Lost

The emphasis of this lesson:

Jesus is a magnificent artisan who knows how to bring total restoration to every part of our lives. Satan is a thief who comes to steal, kill, and destroy anything he can, but Jesus came to give us a life of overflowing abundance. When you're living the abundant life Christ provides, it overflows into the lives of others, touching them in indescribable ways.

There were many places completely destroyed during the Second World War, including the Gatchina Palace located on the outskirts of Saint Petersburg, Russia. Years later, restorers came and worked tirelessly to renovate this Russian landmark and returned it to its original beauty, bringing back to life that which was lost.

In the same way, when Jesus comes into our life, His Spirit takes up permanent residence inside us and goes to work restoring all that was lost to the enemy's attacks. Whatever areas we open to Him, He will fully restore and make brand new by His mighty power!

An Illustration of Restoration

When Rick and Denise Renner first arrived in the former Soviet Union, their family settled in Latvia, a former Soviet Republic. After living in a little village for some time, they decided to move into the city of Riga, the capital of Latvia, which had a population of about 800,000 at that time. Although living space was hard to come by, they managed to find a large, vacant apartment that was available. Unfortunately, it was completely dilapidated and needed a total makeover.

When the Soviets came to power in 1917, they confiscated people's property and moved multiple families into single, common spaces. Apparently, at one time this apartment housed eight different families, and it only had one kitchen and one bathroom. Needless to say, after over 50 years of neglect, it had fallen into shambles. The walls were covered with mold, the ceilings were collapsing, the parquet floors were rotting, and most of the windows were broken, allowing the cold air to pour in. Moreover, all the walls of the apartment had been vandalized with foul words.

As dilapidated as the old place was, Rick was able to see great potential in it. When he looked at the fireplaces and crown molding, he saw hints of its former beauty and believed that with great effort and proper care, things could be restored to its original brilliance. So he and Denise bought the place and went to work renovating every square inch, making it shine once again.

This is a perfect illustration of Jesus' restoration of our life. He is a magnificent artisan who rolls up His sleeves and goes to work immediately, restoring our soul to its original strength and purpose.

Jesus Knows How the Enemy Operates

In John 10:10, Jesus said, "The thief cometh not, but for to steal, and to kill, and to destroy: I am come that they might have life, and that they might have it more abundantly." It may be that you've heard this verse before, but do you know its full meaning? Here, Jesus reveals how the enemy works and contrasts it with His desire to bring us into the abundant life He died to provide.

The devil is a *thief*. This word "thief" is the Greek word *kleptes*, and it describes *a bandit, thief*, or *scam artist*. The word *kleptes* is where we get the term "kleptomaniac," which is one who cannot resist the urge to steal. Make no mistake: Jesus is calling Satan a *kleptomaniac*.

Keep in mind, Jesus has had a great deal of experience with how the enemy works. He was in Heaven and saw firsthand how Lucifer was lifted up in pride and sought to steal the throne of God. But all his plots and plans to take the Father's place in the "sides of the north" and receive the worship of the angels came to a screeching halt when he was kicked out of Heaven (*see* Isaiah 14:12-15; Luke 10:18). When Satan couldn't unseat God and steal His position of authority, he went to work in the Garden of Eden, attempting to s*teal* Adam's position of authority on the earth — only this time, he was successful.

The devil loves to *steal*. Jesus said, "The thief cometh not, but for to steal…" (John 10:10). In Greek, the word "steal" is *klepto*, and it describes *one so artful in the way he steals that his exploits of thievery are nearly* *undetectable.* It depicts *a pickpocket* and, again, is where we get the word "kleptomaniac." Although the word "steal" — *klepto* — is very similar to *kleptes,* the word for "thief," it is the active form and describes his *actions of thievery.* Thus, the first part of John 10:10 could be translated: "*The kleptomaniac, when he shows up, will begin to behave like a kleptomaniac. He can't restrain himself. He'll steal, steal, steal just because it is his nature to steal.*"

This tells us that when the enemy attacks, it may not even be about you. He just wants what you have because that's his nature. For example, if you're healthy, he wants your health. If you're married, he wants your marriage. If you've got a good job, he wants it, and if you have children, he wants them. It doesn't matter what it is; he just wants whatever is yours.

Again, when the devil shows up, he operates like *a bandit, a thief,* or *a scam artist.* He's so *artful in the way he steals that his exploits of thievery are nearly undetectable.* Very artfully and seductively he tries to take everything you have.

Satan also comes to kill. At first glance, you may think this word refers to murder, slaughter, or bloodshed. However, the Greek term for "kill" here is the word *thuo,* which doesn't mean to murder, but *to sacrifice.* It's a First Century religious word that means *to sacrifice, surrender, or to give up something precious and dear.* It was the same word that would have been used among the Greeks when they made sacrifices to their gods — or even among the Jews when they sacrificed something to God.

Jesus is teaching us that the devil can disguise himself to sound very religious — even pretending to be God Himself. This means if we have anything left over after his first acts of stealing from us, he may try to speak to us in religious terms and say, "*You know what? There's no hope of recovery, and there's no way you'll ever be able to restore what you've lost. Why keep on believing? You might as well give it up and lay it all on the altar. Just sacrifice it and walk away.*"

Friend, the devil is a killer who wants you to lay down your promises, your dreams, and everything dear that remains in your life so that he can continue working his evil schemes to devastate and obliterate you. To successfully see through his strategies, you need to get to know the voice of God, which is inseparably connected with the words of Scripture. When you're spending time in the Bible and know what it says, you can recognize when it is Satan speaking and when it is God speaking.

Satan also comes to destroy. The word "destroy" that Jesus used in John 10:10 is a translation of the Greek word *apollumi*, which means *to ruin, waste, trash, devastate*, or *destroy*. Just like the apartment that Rick and Denise purchased was completely trashed and had fallen into shambles, the devil wants to bring complete devastation to any area of your life that he can get his hands on.

First, he tries to *steal (klepto)* whatever he can steal from you — your health, your marriage, your kids, your finances, your future. If you have it, he wants to take it. Satan is a kleptomaniac, and stealing is in his DNA. If he can't steal what's precious to you, next he'll try to convince you to *sacrifice* and *surrender* it (*thuo*) to him. He wants you to believe that the things you treasure are beyond restoration and can never be fixed. Ultimately, his intention is to *destroy (apollumi)* you and leave you in shambles.

What's interesting is the word destroy — *apollumi* — comes from the root *luo*, which means *to loosen* or *to loose*. It is used in Luke 3:16 when John the Baptist said of Jesus, "…But one mightier than I cometh, the latchet of whose shoes I am not worthy to unloose…." The word "unloose" here is the Greek word *luo*, which is part of the word *apollumi*, the word for "destroy" in John 10:10. Again, *apollumi* describes something that is *ruined, unraveled, undone, devastated, trashed, destroyed*, or *completely liquidated*.

Think about what happens when you "unloose" someone's shoes. They can become so loose that they begin to unravel and fall off. By using this word, Jesus tells us that the devil's ultimate intention is to devastate you, trash you, and unravel you to the point that you are completely undone. That is the idea implied in the Greek word *apollumi*.

Taking into account the original Greek meanings, here is the *Renner Interpretive Version (RIV)* of the first part of John 10:10:

> **The thief wants to get his hands into every good thing in your life. In fact, this pickpocket is looking for any opportunity to wiggle his way so deeply into your personal affairs that he can walk off with everything you hold precious and dear. And that's not all. When he's finished stealing all your goods and possessions, he'll take his plan to rob you blind to the next level by creating conditions and situations so horrible that you'll see no way to solve the problems except to sacrifice everything that remains from previous attacks. The goal of this thief is to totally**

devastate your life. If nothing stops him, he'll leave you insolvent, flat broke, and cleaned out in every area of your life. You'll end up feeling as if you're finished and out of business. Make no mistake. The enemy's ultimate aim is to obliterate you.

Jesus Came To Give You 'Abundant Life'

Thankfully, Jesus doesn't just tell us about the enemy's actions. He also tells us why He Himself came. In John 10:10, He went on to say, "…I am come that they might have life, and that they might have it more abundantly." The word "life" here is the Greek word *zoe*, which describes *life filled with zest and vitality*. That's what Jesus came to give you — a life filled with *vitality*.

And the word "abundantly" in Greek is *perissos*, which means *abundantly, excessively, exceedingly*, or *extraordinary*. It describes something that abounds in an extraordinary measure and is so profuse that it can be likened to a river overflowing and flooding beyond its banks. This is the kind of life Jesus has made available to you — a life that's *overflowing, plentiful*, and even *superabundant*.

When you're living the abundant life Christ provides, it overflows into the lives of others around you, touching them in indescribable ways.

Taking into account the original Greek meaning of these words, here is the *Renner Interpretive Version (RIV)* of the second part of John 10:10:

> But I have specifically come with the express purpose that you will have, hold, and possess a phenomenal and amazing life. My purpose is that you will possess life so full that it overflows and spills over like a mighty river so full of water that its banks can no longer contain it all. I'm talking about an amazingly full, spirited, and vivacious life that is literally overflowing and spilling over. I have explicitly come so you can possess an abundant, profuse, plentiful, and bountiful life.

Friend, if there's an area of your life where the enemy has come to steal, kill, and destroy, that is the area that Jesus wants to touch, restore, and bring His abundant life! Surrender yourself to Him, and He will take what is desolate, devastated, and in shambles and make it new again!

STUDY QUESTIONS

Study to shew thyself approved unto God, a workman that needeth not to be ashamed, rightly dividing the word of truth.
— 2 Timothy 2:15

1. Jesus has had a great deal of experience with seeing how the enemy works. According to Isaiah 14:12-15, what exactly did Lucifer do that got him kicked out of Heaven? What was his attitude and mindset that led to his demise? How did God judge him? (Also consider Ezekiel 28:12-19; Luke 10:18.)

2. To successfully see through Satan's strategies, you need to get to know the voice of God, which is inseparably connected with the words of Scripture. What do Hebrews 4:12; James 1:21, and Second Timothy 3:15-17 say the Word of God will produce in your life? What practical steps can you take to take in more of God's Word regularly?

PRACTICAL APPLICATION

But be ye doers of the word, and not hearers only, deceiving your own selves.
— James 1:22

1. The enemy is a kleptomaniac — trying to steal everything in sight is ingrained in his DNA. What has the enemy been working overtime to steal from you? How about your family?

2. In your own words, briefly describe the meaning of the words *steal*, *kill*, and *destroy*. What new eye-opening insights did you learn about these three modes of operation Satan uses?

3. Is there an area in your life where the devil has disguised himself to sound like God and is trying to get you to sacrifice something that is precious? If so, what has he been trying to get you to give up? How does this lesson embolden you to stand your ground against him?

TOPIC
Jesus Can Restore You From Any Abuse You Have Experienced

SCRIPTURES

1. **Ephesians 2:2-5** — Wherein in time past ye walked according to the course of this world, according to the prince of the power of the air, the spirit that now worketh in the children of disobedience: Among whom also we all had our conversation in times past.... But God, who is rich in mercy, for his great love wherewith he loved us. Even when we were dead in sins, [God] hath quickened us together with Christ, (by grace ye are saved).

2. **Ephesians 2:10** — For we are his workmanship, created in Christ Jesus unto good works, which God hath before ordained that we should walk in them.

GREEK WORDS

1. "in time past" — ἐν αἷς ποτε (*en hais pote*): it means "back then"

2. "according to" — κατά (*kata*): a downward force; domination or sub-jugation; controlled by

3. "course" — κόσμος (*kosmos*): conveys ideas of order and arrange-ment; describes society because it is a system that possesses order and arrangement; also carries with it the ideas of fashion and sophistication

4. "world" — αἰῶνος (*aionos*): an age with a concrete beginning and a concrete ending; a measurable and limited period of time, like a cen-tury or decade or generation

5. "the prince" — τὸν ἄρχοντα (*ton archonta*): from ἄρχων (*archon*) with a definite article; the prince, the ruler, the preeminent authority figure; the one with influence and jurisdiction in a particular realm

6. "worketh" — ἐνεργοῦντος (*energountos*): from ἐνεργέω (*energeo*), energy; a power that energizes or activates; depicts a powerful force that is set into motion; active power; here, an energizing presence

7. "disobedience" — ἀπείθεια (*apeitheia*): πείθω (*peitho*) and an ἀ (*a*) affixed to it; when transformed into ἀπειθής (*apeithes*), it means unpersuadable, uncontrollable, or unleadable; belligerent; non-compliant; obstinate; no longer able to persuade, control, lead, or exercise authority over; rebellious

8. "conversation" — ἀναστρέφω (*anastrepho*): lifestyle; portrays one's rising up and sitting down

9. "in times past" — ποτε (*pote*): at that time; back then

10. "but" — δὲ (*de*): an emphatic marker to emphasize the next statement

11. "rich" — πλούσιος (*plousios*): wealth so great it cannot be tabulated; abundant wealth; vast wealth; extreme riches; incredible abundance; magnificent opulence; extravagant lavishness; used by Plato to say no one was richer than legendary King Midas

12. "mercy" — ἔλεος (*eleos*): pity; compassion; a heart-wrenching emotion that compels one to action

13. "great" — πολύς (*polus*): depicts something so great that it is incalculable

14. "workmanship" — ποίημα (*poiema*): poem; product; a thing made; workmanship

15. "created" — κτίζω (*ktidzo*): creation of something from nothing; not renewed or refashioned with old material, but brand-spanking new and never existing before; not enhanced, improved, repaired, or restored; something newly created and original

SYNOPSIS

The Gatchina Palace, which is located in Saint Petersburg, Russia, was once the seat for the imperial Romanov family. However, during WWII Nazi troops invaded the region, bombing and pillaging the palace until it was totally decimated. After many years, restorers united their efforts and began renovating this historic building back to its original condition.

Spiritually speaking, God is the restorer of all things. Wherever your life is broken down and decimated is exactly where He desires to go to work and bring restoration. Do you need healing in your body, reconciliation in your relationships, or revitalization in your finances? Invite Jesus to begin working in your life to bring full restoration.

The emphasis of this lesson:

Before the grace of God touched our lives, we were dominated, manipulated, and controlled by the whims of the world and Satan himself. He is the energizing force working through society and in the children of disobedience. But God who is immeasurably rich in mercy, demonstrated His great love by saving us and making us alive in Christ. We are His masterpiece!

What We Were Like *Before* Jesus Saved Us

Each and every one of us has a story to tell about our lives — a story that pictures us both before and after Jesus touched our lives. The fact is that all of us have been mistreated, rejected, and abused in some way or another and have need of Jesus' restorative touch. That is what the apostle Paul talks about in his letter to the Ephesian believers. He said:

> **Wherein in time past ye walked according to the course of this world, according to the prince of the power of the air, the spirit that now worketh in the children of disobedience.**
> **— Ephesians 2:2**

Notice the phrase "in time past" — the words *en hais pote* in Greek. It means "back then" and is the equivalent of Paul saying, "Let's think back to what we were like *back then*, when we were spiritually dead." It's almost as if Paul took out his wallet and pulled out a picture of what we used to look like *before* we were saved by God's grace to remind us of what we looked like.

Basically, he said, "Back then…before Jesus touched and began to transform our life, we all walked 'according to the course of this world.'" The words "according to" are a translation of the Greek word *kata*, which describes *a downward force; something that is dominating, subjugating,* or *controlling*. Thus, before we were saved, our lives were *dominated, controlled,* and even *manipulated* by "the course of this world."

In Greek, the word "course" here is *kosmos*, which conveys the ideas of *order* and *arrangement*. This word was also used to describe *society* because it is a system that possesses order and arrangement. Moreover, the word *kosmos* also carries with it the ideas of *fashion* and *sophistication*.

Hence, before the grace of God touched our lives, we were dominated, manipulated, and controlled by society around us — by the news, the education system, entertainment, fashionable trends, and even the government. Whatever the whims of culture were dictating, we fluctuated and flowed with its standards.

This brings us to the word "world," which is actually a very poor translation. In this verse, the word "world" is the Greek word *aionos*, and it describes *an age with a concrete beginning and a concrete ending*. It is *a measurable and limited period of time, like a century or decade or generation*. Again, Paul was telling us that those who are unsaved don't have an eternal perspective; they live by the fluctuating views or whims of the age in which they live. Whatever way the winds of society are blowing, that's the way they think.

Satan Is the Energizing Presence Manipulating and Dominating the World

Not only did we think and act according to the whims of society, but also "…according to the prince of the power of the air…" (Ephesians 2:2). Once more, we see the phrase "according to" — the Greek word *kata* — which describes *a downward force* or *something that is dominating and subjugating*. It is something so powerful in its manipulation that it controls those under its influence.

In this case, Paul reveals that there is a spiritual force behind this dominating influence, and it is "the prince of the power of the air." The phrase "the prince" is *ton archonta* in Greek. It is from the term *archon* and has a definite article with it. Hence, this is not just any prince. It denotes *the prince, the ruler*, or *the preeminent authority figure*. It is *the one with influence and jurisdiction in a particular realm*.

The controlling force that is manipulating and dominating the unsaved is "the prince of the power of the air," who is Satan. Although he doesn't have authority over the universe or over nature, he does have authority in the realm of the world's systems, working through people and the whims of the times. He uses things like governments, entertainment, education, religious organizations, and the court system to achieve his agenda. It is why he is called "the god of this world" in Second Corinthians 4:4.

Paul went on to say that Satan "…now worketh in the children of disobedience" (Ephesians 2:2). The word "worketh" is the Greek word *energountos*, which is from *energeo*, the term for *energy*. This word describes *a power that energizes or activates*. It depicts *a powerful force that is set into motion* or *an active power*. In this verse, it signifies *an energizing presence*. Hence, Satan is the energizing presence working through society and in the "children of disobedience."

The word "disobedience" in this verse is the Greek word *apeitheia*. It is derived from the word *peitho*, which means *to be persuaded or convinced*. But when an "a" is affixed to the front of it and it becomes *apeithes*, it describes *one who is unpersuadable, uncontrollable*, or *unleadable*. This is a person who is *belligerent, non-compliant*, and *obstinate*. He or she is *no longer able to be persuaded, controlled, or led*. This person is *rebellious* and will not submit to authority. This is a clear picture of Satan's ultimate goal: to create a world system filled with people who are obstinate and rebellious to the principles and standards of God's Word.

We Were Born With a Sin Nature and Had the Capacity To Sin Big

Keep in mind what Paul has been describing in Ephesians 2:2 is not just a picture of unbelievers — it is also a vivid snapshot of who we used to be before we were saved. The moment we entered the world, we were born into sin and had a sin nature. Although you may not have reached the full potential of immorality and sinfulness, you had that potential because you had the nature of sin. In fact, the Bible says you were a slave to sin (*see* Romans 6:20), and Satan, the god of this world, was controlling your life. According to Ephesians 2:2, the enemy himself was energizing you, driving you and manipulating your life. It's no wonder you experienced abuse, bondage, and pain in your past — Satan was running the show in your life.

Paul confirms this by saying, "Among whom also we all had our conversation in times past…" (Ephesians 2:3). The word "conversation" here is the Greek word *anastrepho*, and it describes *a lifestyle*. It portrays *one's rising up and sitting down, one's going in and going out*. And the phrase "in times past" is a translation of the Greek word *pote*, which means *at that time* or *back then*. Essentially, Paul is reminding us that our entire lifestyle before coming to Christ was under the influence of the enemy.

But God…

Thankfully, Paul didn't leave us hopelessly focused on who we used to be. Instead, he flipped the script and began to speak about the indescribable compassion of God. He said, "But God, who is rich in mercy, for his great love wherewith he loved us, even when we were dead in sins, [God] hath quickened us together with Christ, (by grace ye are saved)" (Ephesians 2:4,5).

There are several important words to understand in this verse, including the word "but," which is the Greek word *de*. It is used as *an emphatic marker* to emphasize the next important statement:

'God, Rich in Mercy'

The word "rich" in Greek is simply fabulous! It is the word *plousios*, and it describes *wealth so great it cannot be tabulated*. It signifies *abundant wealth*, *vast wealth, extreme riches, incredible abundance, magnificent opulence*, and *extravagant lavishness*. It is the very word used by Plato to say no one was richer than legendary King Midas.

In context of Ephesians 2:4, Paul informs us that God is "rich in mercy." This means He has so much mercy it cannot be tabulated! His supply is incredibly abundant and extravagantly lavish. What is "mercy"? It is the Greek word *eleos*, which describes *pity* or *compassion*; it is *a heart-wrenching emotion that compels one to action*.

Real mercy doesn't just look at someone or something and say, "Oh, that's so sad." Instead, mercy says, "I'm going to do something to help bring change." A careful study of Scripture reveals that when God saw us in our unsaved, sin-sick condition, His immeasurable mercy moved Him to swing into action! We might say that when it comes to mercy, God is filthy, stinking rich (*plousios*).

Through His mercy and love, He stepped in and changed our condition, bringing us out of our miserable mess and into the light of His Kingdom. Paul says God's love is "great," which is the Greek word *polus*, and it depicts *something so great that it is incalculable*. Thus, God's love for you is beyond measure, limitless.

How did God demonstrate His incalculable love for you? Ephesians 2:5 says, "Even when we were dead in sins, [God] hath quickened us together with Christ, (by grace ye are saved)." The word "dead" here is the Greek word *nekros*, which is the term for *a lifeless corpse*. It has no pulse or heartbeat, no breath in its lungs, no desires, and no ability to make decisions. The use of this word tells us that before we were saved, we were like a spiritual *corpse* — we couldn't even think about going after God. Thus, our salvation had nothing to do with us and everything to do with Him.

You Are God's 'Masterpiece'

Paul went on to say in Ephesians 2:10, "For we are his workmanship, created in Christ Jesus unto good works, which God hath before ordained that we should walk in them." One of the most important words in this passage is the word "workmanship." It is the Greek word *poiema*, and it describes *a poem, a product*, or *a thing made*. It is actually the word for *a masterpiece* and carries the idea of *something that is artfully created*. It denotes *one who has the ability to write or create a literary masterpiece*.

This word *poiema* explains what happened when you became a child of God, and it emphatically means that on the day you got saved, God put forth His most powerful and creative effort to make you new. Once God finished making you new, you became *a masterpiece*, skillfully and artfully created in Christ Jesus. Hence, God's creative, artistic, intelligent genius went into your making.

The word "created" in Ephesians 2:10 is the Greek word *ktidzo*, and it describes *the creation of something from nothing*. It is not something renewed or refashioned with old material, but *brand-spanking new and never existing before*. It is not something enhanced, improved, repaired, or restored; it is *something newly created and original*.

This tells us that when God took us from the world of abuse — a world where we were dominated by sin and controlled by the prince of the power of the air — He quickened us together in Christ even when we were not looking at or thinking of Him. We were dead (*nekros*) in our sins — a lifeless corpse spiritually. Yet, God saw us and wanted us. He chose us and made us alive in Christ, giving us ears to hear the gospel and eyes to see that we needed to be saved. The instant we said *yes* to God, the Holy Spirit moved inside us and went to work, using His power and all of His brilliance to make us a creative masterpiece (a *poiema*).

Friend, you are God's *poem* — a literary masterpiece of His incalculable love and mercy. He has not only touched your life, but also changed your story. It doesn't matter what was written about you before. The masterful Creator rewrote the story of your life and gave you a new ending. He created you to be His workmanship or His masterpiece — marvelously recreated in Christ Jesus!

STUDY QUESTIONS

Study to shew thyself approved unto God, a workman that needeth not to be ashamed, rightly dividing the word of truth.
— 2 Timothy 2:15

1. Do you know — really and personally know — that God loves you? What does Romans 5:8 and First John 4:9,10 say is the proof of God's boundless love for you? Ask the Holy Spirit to give you a fresh revelation of God's love.

2. Ephesians 2:10 (*NLT*) says, "For we are God's *masterpiece* ...." When God looks at you, *He sees Jesus.* He's not looking at your behavior or the areas you may be struggling with sin. He is focused on who you are *in Christ.* What else does the Bible say God is thinking about you and doing? Read and meditate on the following verses:

   • **1 John 3:1 and John 1:12,13**

   • **1 Peter 2:9 and Isaiah 61:6**

   • **2 Corinthians 5:21 and Ephesians 1:4**

   • **Psalm 139:17,18 and Jeremiah 29:11**

   • **Zephaniah 3:17**

PRACTICAL APPLICATION

But be ye doers of the word, and not hearers only, deceiving your own selves.
— James 1:22

1. Each of us has a story to tell about our lives. If you had 30 seconds to share a snapshot of who you were *before* Jesus came into your life, what would you say? Likewise, if you had the chance to testify about how God has *transformed* your life, what would you share?

2. People who are not saved (unbelievers) are dominated, manipulated, and controlled by the whims of society and Satan, the god of this world. He uses the news, the education system, entertainment, fash-

ionable trends, and even the government to dictate what people do. Be honest: are you being led by the Holy Spirit or are you being more influenced and manipulated by the dictates of culture? What evidence in your life confirms your answer?

3. When it comes to mercy, the Bible says that God has so much of it that it is incalculable! When you look at your life, in what specific ways has God shown you mercy? Why not take time now to *thank* Him and *praise* Him for blessing you in such marvelous ways!

LESSON 3

TOPIC
Jesus Can Masterfully Restore You

SCRIPTURES

1. **Psalm 23:1-3** — The Lord is my shepherd; I shall not want. He maketh me to lie down in green pastures: He leadeth me beside the still waters. He restoreth my soul....

2. **Jeremiah 30:17** (*NKJV*) — For I will restore health to you and heal you of your wounds, says the Lord....

3. **John 10:10** — The thief cometh not, but for to steal, and to kill, and to destroy: I am come that they might have life, and that they might have it more abundantly.

4. **Luke 19:10** — For the Son of man is come to seek and to save that which was lost.

GREEK WORDS

1. "lost" — ἀπολωλός (*apololos*): derived from the word *apollumi*, and it conveys the idea of something ruined, wasted, trashed, devastated, or destroyed; the same word for the Destroyer — one of the New Testament names to describe Satan's demented nature

2. "seek" — ζητέω (*zeteo*): to desire, to pursue, seek, or earnestly search for; a person so intent on achieving his goal that he will search, seek, and investigate, never giving up in his pursuit to get what he wants

3. "save" — σῴζω (*sodzo*): implies rescue, such as a rescue from a raging sea, rescue from an illness, rescue from immediate danger; inherent in this type of "rescue" is one's return to safety and soundness

SYNOPSIS

Located just outside Saint Petersburg, Russia, is the renowned Gatchina Palace, boasting of nearly 600 rooms designed by celebrated Italian architect Antonio Rinaldi. We know from history it was gifted by Catherine the Great to her boyfriend Count Orlov, and when Orlov died in 1807, she purchased it back and gave it to her son Paul I, who eventually became the emperor of Russia.

After being in the royal family for many generations, Gatchina was bombed and burned by Nazi troops in WWII, bringing great devastation and destruction. Once the war was over, the fortress was used briefly for military purposes, and then restorers went to work in the mid-1970s to reinstate the palace's original beauty and magnificence.

The restoration of this historic landmark is a reminder of how Jesus brings restoration to our lives. The Bible says, "For the Son of man is come to seek and to save that which was lost" (Luke 19:10). Whatever has been damaged, destroyed, or lost in your life as a result of the enemy's efforts, Jesus wants to restore. But He can only renovate what you give Him access to. If you will surrender the broken areas of your life to Him, He'll begin revitalizing things and putting them in order.

The emphasis of this lesson:

All of us have experienced various forms of insult, abuse, neglect, disappointment, and mistreatment. The good news is God is in the restoration business and can heal all our wounds and the pain the enemy has inflicted. When Jesus — the Great Artisan — lays His hands on our life, He releases His divine power, restoring what the devil has damaged or destroyed, making it better than it ever was!

The Lord Restores Our Soul

The theme of God being our restorer is something we see all through Scripture. One of the most powerful declarations of restoration is found in the book of Psalms where David writes:

The Lord is my shepherd; I shall not want. He maketh me to lie down in green pastures: He leadeth me beside the still waters. He restoreth my soul....

— Psalm 23:1-3

If there is one thing we can all agree on, it is that we're living in a broken world, and it can often take its toll on our lives. The truth is all of us have experienced various hurts and pains from others. Insults, abuse, neglect, disappointments, and mistreatments of all kinds have left multiple wounds in our souls. The good news is God is in the restoration business! Through the prophet Jeremiah, He tells us:

For I will restore health to you and heal you of your wounds, says the Lord....

— Jeremiah 30:17 (*NKJV*)

When life bruises and afflicts us, the Holy Spirit is ready and willing to heal and restore. It is an inseparable part of God's nature.

Jesus Was and Is the Great Artisan

Before Jesus entered into ministry, the Gospel writers tell us He was a *carpenter* (*see* Matthew 13:55; Mark 6:3). Unfortunately, this is a very poor translation. In the original Greek, the word "carpenter" is *teknos*, which is from where we get the words *technology* and *technician*. Although this word can describe *a person who made sophisticated furniture of wood veneers inlaid with ivory and precious stones*, a broader and more accurate translation would be someone who was *a master craftsman*.

Thus, a person who was a *teknos* was also one who worked with gold, silver, and bronze and fashioned dazzling jewelry. Likewise, it was someone who painted frescos on the walls of buildings or who was so artistic he could design and install frescos made of marble. Furthermore, this word *teknos* was used in the literary world to describe men who were so brilliant that they could write literary masterpieces.

In light of this word's use and its meaning, we could translate the term *teknos* as *one who has the ability to produce or to bring forth great things*. If we chose one word to sum up what a *teknos* is, we would likely choose the word *artisan*. That's what Jesus was — and *is* — the Great Artisan. Every person's life that He touched He made shine with His glory, and He is still doing that today. When He lays His hands on our life, He releases

His divine power, restoring what the devil has damaged or destroyed, making it better than it ever was!

A Picture of Real-Life Restoration

To help us have a better understanding of what it means to restore something, Rick went into more detail about the restoration project that he and Denise undertook in their early years of living in Riga, the capital of Latvia. If you remember, they had been living in a little village and had decided to move to the city. They didn't have much money, and good living spaces were hard to come by. After searching diligently, Rick found an old, dilapidated apartment on the second floor of a vacated building that was constructed in 1898. At one time, it was one of the most exquisite buildings in Riga's most prestigious neighborhoods, but after 55 years of communism, the whole area had become dilapidated.

You may recall the movie *Dr. Zhivago* in which the doctor returned to his home after communism came to power, and he found that his once luxurious residence had been confiscated and subdivided into multiple family dwellings. That is exactly what had taken place with the apartment the Renners were considering to purchase in Riga. Eight families had been placed in this space, forced into sharing its thirteen rooms, seven fireplaces, one kitchen, and one bathroom.

The day Rick walked into the place, the ceilings were collapsing, the plastered walls were crumbling, the windows were broken out, and mold was growing everywhere. Urine had saturated the floor in the bathroom for so long it had eaten a hole straight through so that you could see the apartment below. To top it off, hooligans had painted derogatory words and nasty phrases all over the walls throughout the apartment. It was shameful to see what had happened to this once-luxurious apartment where an elite class of people had formerly lived.

Although dirt, grime, filth, and trash were heaped in huge piles in every room, Rick knew the place could be beautiful again if they would be willing to do what was necessary to bring it back to its former glory. Amazingly, even under 55 years of botched paint jobs, he was able to see glimpses of restored crown molding, glistening high ceilings, and lavish fireplaces so spectacular that they should be on display in a museum.

Because of the apartment's condemned state, it was available for a low price, and once the Renners purchased it, they immediately went to work restoring it. Little by little, new life was infused into every crack and crevice. From the painted-over parquet floors and mold-laden walls to the crumbling, collapsed ceilings and broken windows, every facet of the place was worked on and overhauled. Even the crown molding, which had been covered by more than 50 years of white, chalk-like Soviet paint, was brought back to life. An expert came in and used dental instruments to clean every little detail in the crown molding until one day it emerged in its original magnificence.

After almost a year of nonstop work, the dilapidated apartment was amazingly restored to its former glory. Because Rick and Denise accepted the challenge and restored the property, they were rewarded with something very glorious and magnificent that emerged from what was once ravaged, wasted, and devastated. In fact, the renovated version was probably even more beautiful than the original.

When we think about the dreadful condition of that apartment in Riga and all the work that was required to restore it, it is a great example of the in-depth restoration that is needed to restore a human life. Although Satan and his imps are in the destruction business, always seeking to trash people's lives, Jesus is in the restoration business, and He will renew every room in our life we give Him access to.

There's a Big Difference Between How Satan Works and Jesus Works

Looking once more at Jesus' words in John 10:10, He said, "The thief cometh not, but for to steal, and to kill, and to destroy: I am come that they might have life, and that they might have it more abundantly." In our first lesson, we learned how the devil deviously works to bring devastation to our life and how Jesus stands ready and willing to bless our life with abundance.

Taking into account the original Greek meaning of the words in this passage, here once more is the *Renner Interpretive Version (RIV)* of John 10:10:

> **The thief wants to get his hands into every good thing in your life. In fact, this pickpocket is looking for any opportunity to wiggle his way so deeply into your personal affairs that he can walk off with everything you hold precious and dear. And**

that's not all. When he's finished stealing all your goods and possessions, he'll take his plan to rob you blind to the next level by creating conditions and situations so horrible that you'll see no way to solve the problems except to sacrifice everything that remains from previous attacks. The goal of this thief is to totally devastate your life. If nothing stops him, he'll leave you insolvent, flat broke, and cleaned out in every area of your life. You'll end up feeling as if you're finished and out of business. Make no mistake. The enemy's ultimate aim is to obliterate you.

But I have specifically come with the express purpose that you will have, hold, and possess a phenomenal and amazing life. My purpose is that you will possess life so full that it overflows and spills over like a mighty river so full of water that its banks can no longer contain it all. I'm talking about an amazingly full, spirited, and vivacious life that is literally overflowing and spilling over. I have explicitly come so you can possess an abundant, profuse, plentiful, and bountiful life.

Friend, whatever Satan has tried to steal, kill, or destroy in your life, Jesus has the power to restore it! Just as Rick and Denise rolled up their sleeves and began to peel back over five decades of Soviet wallpaper and paint from their walls, Jesus will go to work in you — peeling back and removing the hurt and dirt of your past life one layer at a time. Nothing is too difficult for Him!

Jesus Came 'To Seek and Save That Which Was Lost'

Jesus was God in the flesh (see John 1:14), and when He came to earth, His mission was clear. In Luke 19:10 He said, "For the Son of man is come to seek and to save that which was lost." There are three key words we need to understand in order to better grasp the meaning of His mission, and those words are *seek*, *save*, and *lost*.

The word "lost" is the Greek word *apololos*. It is derived from the word *apollumi*, which conveys the idea of something *ruined, wasted, trashed, devastated*, or *destroyed*. It is the same word for the *Destroyer* — one of the New Testament names to describe Satan's demented nature.

Although the word "lost" in Luke 19:10 refers to Jesus' mission to seek and save unbelievers, it also indicates His intention is to seek and save the areas of loss in our lives, such as broken relationships, abusive childhoods, and a loss of identity. Keep in mind, the word "lost" (*apololos*) describes *anything that has become unraveled to the point that it falls to pieces.* If there are things in your life the enemy has worked to steal, kill, and destroy and you've become unraveled, you are a perfect candidate for God's restoration project!

The word **"seek"** is the Greek word *zeteo*, which means *to desire, to pursue, to seek,* or *earnestly search for.* It pictures a person so intent on achieving his goal that he will search, seek, and investigate, never giving up in his pursuit to get what he wants. The use of this word signifies that Jesus *has put forth* and *is putting forth* His best efforts to actively seek, save, and restore whatever Satan has tried to steal, kill, or destroy.

The word **"save"** is the Greek word *sodzo*, which is the most common word for *salvation* in the New Testament. It implies *rescue,* such as *a rescue from a raging sea, rescue from an illness,* or *rescue from immediate danger.* Inherent in this type of "rescue" is one's return to safety and soundness. Thus, Jesus' work to save us isn't just a *salvage operation* — it's *a full-scale rescue* that results in a *redemptive* and *fully restorative operation.*

To be clear: When Christ finishes His work in us, we are *not* a weaker, substandard version of what we were before. On the contrary, we're stronger, better, and more improved because of what Jesus has done to *rescue* us and to *redeem* and *restore* our hearts and lives to a state of wholeness in Him! We are *not* a second-rate version of something we used to be. In Christ, we are filled with the full potential of the Holy Spirit who lives inside us.

Although Rick and Denise never saw the original state of the apartment that was built in Riga in 1898, they were able to compare the completely restored version to the condition it was in when they first found it, and the transformation was absolutely amazing! How could such a horrible, dilapidated place become beautiful and whole again? It was the result of faith, imagination, hard work, and a lot of prayer. It didn't happen overnight. It was a daily effort. With hard work, faith, prayer, and the help of others, the results were breathtaking!

Likewise, Jesus is seeking to perform a rescue operation in every area of *your* life where Satan has attempted to bring devastation and ruin. He also seeks to rescue and restore those around you who need rescuing. Don't give up on what He's doing in you or in them, because rescue operations are Jesus' specialty!

STUDY QUESTIONS

Study to shew thyself approved unto God, a workman that needeth not to be ashamed, rightly dividing the word of truth.
— 2 Timothy 2:15

1. The Bible says that before starting His ministry, Jesus was a "carpenter," which is a translation of the Greek word *teknos*. Prior to this lesson, what did you understand this word to mean? How do you see it differently now, and how has your appreciation of Jesus' work in your life increased?

2. Luke 19:10 tells us that Jesus came to earth to *seek and save that which was lost*. According to First John 3:8 and Hebrews 2:14, what was another primary purpose of His ministry?

PRACTICAL APPLICATION

But be ye doers of the word, and not hearers only, deceiving your own selves.
— James 1:22

1. What are some of the biggest *before* and *after* changes Jesus has made in your life? Consider your attitudes and actions, along with how you talk and think. How has Christ changed you for the better?

2. Rick and Denise's old, dilapidated apartment didn't become beautiful and whole overnight. It took ongoing faith, imagination, hard work, a lot of prayer, and the help of others. What does this practical example tell you about the restoration process in your own life? ·

3. The Lord is your Shepherd who restores your **soul**, which consists of your *mind*, your *will*, and your *emotions*. In what ways do you need the Lord to restore — or *make new* — your thinking, your decision-making ability, and your feelings? If you're not sure, pray and ask the Holy Spirit to show you where you need healing.

TOPIC

Jesus Is in the Restoration Business

SCRIPTURES

1. **Luke 4:16-19** — And he came to Nazareth, where he had been brought up: and, as his custom was, he went into the synagogue on the sabbath day, and stood up for to read. And there was delivered unto him the book of the prophet Esaias. And when he had opened the book, he found the place where it was written, The Spirit of the Lord is upon me, because he hath anointed me to preach the gospel to the poor; he hath sent me to heal the brokenhearted, to preach deliverance to the captives, and recovering of sight to the blind, to set at liberty them that are bruised, to preach the acceptable year of the Lord.

GREEK WORDS

1. "poor" — πτωχός (*ptochos*): abject poverty or those who are impoverished; thus, Jesus is anointed to set people free who live in abject poverty

2. "heal" — ἰάομαι (*iaomai*): to cure; usually refers to a progressive cure; often depicts a healing power that progressively reverses a condition over a period of time, or a sickness that is progressively healed rather than instantaneously healed

3. "brokenhearted" — συντρίβω (*suntribo*): used to describe the crushing of grapes with the feet, or the smashing and grinding of bones into dust; depicts people who have been walked on by others, those who have been crushed by others, or those who feel they have been smashed to pieces by life or relationships

4. "deliverance" — ἄφεσις (*aphesis*): a release; a dismissal; to set free; to permanently loose

5. "captives" — αἰχμάλωτος (*aichmalotos*): captives; those taken captive at the point of a spear; those who are dragged into bondage; manipulated by bondage

6. "recovery of sight"— ἀνάβλεψις (*anablepsis*): the returning of one's sight; the restoration of sight; to see again

7. "blind"— τυφλός (*tuphlos*): blind; it doesn't just depict a person who is unable to see, but a person who has been intentionally blinded by someone else; can picture one whose eyes have been deliberately removed so that he is blinded; that individual hasn't just lost his sight, but he has no eyes with which to see

8. "set at liberty"— ἄφεσις (*aphesis*): a release; a dismissal; to permanently loose; to set free; in this case, from the detrimental effects of a shattered life; the Greek speaks of a permanent release from the destructive effects of brokenness

9. "bruised"— τεθραυσμένους (*tethrausmenous*): to crush; to break down; depicts a person who has been shattered or fractured by life; pictures those whose lives have been continually split up and fragmented

10. "acceptable"— δεκτός (*dektos*): favorable or accepted; it describes a favorable time to receive; this means when the Lord comes on the scene, it is a divine moment and a favorable time to receive freedom, healing, and restoration for the poor, broken, blind, and anyone that has been traumatized by life

SYNOPSIS

As we have noted in our previous three lessons, the Gatchina Palace is truly magnificent and has been around for over 240 years. After being bombed repeatedly and decimated by enemy troops in WWII, it underwent extensive restoration. Interestingly, restorers made a decision to leave one room of the palace virtually untouched to show the public what the effects of war had done and how powerful the work of restoration can be.

The scale of devastation inflicted on this fortress is a vivid reminder of how Satan and his cohorts come against us as believers. Jesus said, "The thief cometh not, but for to steal, and to kill, and to destroy..." (John 10:10). Ultimately, the enemy wants to totally obliterate your life. In great contrast, Jesus declared, "...I am come that they might have life, and that they might have it more abundantly."

Jesus wants to reverse the effects of the devil's destruction in your life and brilliantly restore everything that's been lost! His work of restoration is miraculous! If you will let Him, He will make your life an inspiration to others, restoring everything *better* than it was before.

The emphasis of this lesson:

Jesus was anointed by the mighty hands of God to carry out six restorative works in people's lives. These include: (1) preaching the Gospel to the poor; (2) healing the brokenhearted; (3) preaching deliverance to the captives; (4) giving recovery of sight to the blind; (5) setting at liberty them that are bruised; and (6) preaching the acceptable year of the Lord.

Jesus Was Anointed
by the Mighty Hands of God

After being baptized by John in the Jordan River and then tested in the wilderness 40 days, the Bible says, "And Jesus returned in the power of the Spirit into Galilee…" (Luke 4:14). It was at that moment He was launched into ministry and began His mission to rescue and restore. Scripture goes on to say, "And he came to Nazareth, where he had been brought up: and, as his custom was, he went into the synagogue on the sabbath day, and stood up for to read" (Luke 4:16). It's important to see that going to the synagogue was Jesus' "custom," which means going to church was a *habit.* If Jesus had a habit of going to church, so should we.

Once inside the synagogue, the Bible says, "…There was delivered unto him the book of the prophet Esaias [Isaiah]. And when he had opened the book, he found the place where it was written, The Spirit of the Lord is upon me, because he hath anointed me to preach the gospel to the poor; he hath sent me to heal the brokenhearted, to preach deliverance to the captives, and recovering of sight to the blind, to set at liberty them that are bruised, to preach the acceptable year of the Lord" (Luke 4:17-19).

The passage Jesus read from here was Isaiah 61:1 and 2 — a passage written about Jesus by the prophet Isaiah over 700 years before He walked the earth. The first thing Jesus said was, "The Spirit of the Lord is *upon* me…" (Luke 4:18). In Greek , the word "upon" is *epi*, and it literally means *upon* or *on top of.* Next, Jesus declared, "…because he hath anointed me…" (Luke 4:18). The word "anointed" is a form of the Greek word *chrio*, which means *to rub, to bathe*, and, in certain contexts, *to massage.* In the Old and

New Testaments, the word "anoint" depicted *a person whose life was touched and empowered by the hands of God.*

When Jesus said, "The Spirit of the Lord is upon me, because he hath anointed me," it was the equivalent of Him saying, "I'm anointed and the reason I'm anointed is because the hand of God is upon me." Make no mistake: it is the mighty hand of God that brings the anointing on our lives. When a person is anointed to teach, to sing, to administrate, or to serve in any way, it is visible evidence that God's hands are upon their life.

What Was Jesus Anointed To Do?

As we carefully read through Jesus' declaration in Luke 4:18, we can identify six specific restorative works that He was anointed by God to do. Let's take a closer look at each of these and unpack the rich meaning found in the original Greek text.

#1: To preach the Gospel to the poor.

The very first action Jesus said He was anointed to carry out was to *preach the gospel to the poor*. Many people have the idea that we're supposed to help the poor by giving them food, clothing, and a financial handout, but that they will always be poor. But there's more that Jesus is saying here. Yes, He wants us to help the poor in practical ways, but the fact of the matter is **the Gospel is an economic game changer.** Wherever it is consistently preached and honored, it improves the financial atmosphere.

Jesus said He was anointed to "preach" to the poor — which literally means to *evangelize* and bring them the Good News. This word "poor" here is the Greek word *ptochos*, and it pictures *abject poverty or those who are impoverished*. This tells us the Gospel is good news for the poor. When Jesus spoke, the anointing of God on His life set people free who were living in abject poverty. Still today, when people hear the Gospel and embrace it, it changes their economic status in life.

If you feel you're financially struggling and living in abject circumstances, Jesus has the power to restore you! If you'll believe and obediently act on what He says in His Word, His truth will bring financial restoration in your life that you never thought was possible.

#2: To heal the brokenhearted.

The next thing Jesus said He was anointed to do was to *heal the broken-hearted.* The fact that Jesus came to heal means that there are many people who have had their health stolen and need it restored. In Greek, there are a few different words for "healing" in the New Testament, such as the word *therapeuo,* which describes *a healing that requires corresponding actions and participation* on the part of the sick person.

In this particular verse, the word "heal" is the Greek word *iaomai,* which literally means *to cure,* and it usually refers to *a progressive cure — a healing power that progressively reverses a condition over a period of time.* In this case, the person's sickness is *progressively healed* rather than healed *instantaneously.* This means that not all healing happens instantaneously; sometimes it happens progressively.

When Jesus said that we would lay hands on the sick and they would recover (*see* Mark 16:18), He used the word *iaomai.* This means if we'll be faithful to pull our hands out of our pockets and lay them on the sick, the Spirit of God will go to work and progressively restore their health. Yes, some people will be instantly healed, but if they're not, we can still know that from the moment we lay hands on them and pray, they will begin to get well.

In Luke 4:18, Jesus specifically said He was anointed to heal the "brokenhearted," which in Greek is the word *suntribo.* This term is used throughout the New Testament and First Century writings to describe *the crushing of grapes with the feet* or *the smashing and grinding of bones into dust.* Here, it depicts *people who have been walked on by others, those who have been crushed by others, or those who feel they have been smashed to pieces by life or relationships.* Thus, the word "brokenhearted" describes those who are *emotionally shattered, tattered,* and *smashed.*

If you feel you've been smashed and crushed by others or fractured by life's circumstances, Jesus has the power to begin to peel back the layers of pain and disappointment and progressively heal you from all the effects of that devastation. Any brokenhearted person who embraces the truth of God's Word will experience this work of restoration in their life. That's God's promise of wholeness in this verse.

#3: To preach deliverance to the captives.

Notice the word "deliverance" in Luke 4:18. It is the Greek word *aphesis*, which describes *a release* or *a dismissal*. It means *to set free* or *to permanently loose*, and this *release* or *permanent freedom* is for the "captives." In Greek, the word "captives" is *aichmalotos*, and it describes *those taken captive at the point of a spear*. It is the picture of a Roman soldier pressing his sharp spear against the back of a captive that is bound in chains.

Think about how you would respond if your hands were bound and someone had a sharp spear pressed between your shoulder blades. You would go wherever that spear directed you to go. This word "captives" pictures an outside force manipulating, forcing, and dragging a person into bondage. Specifically, it represents any kind of addiction that enslaves or controls a person's life. This would include people who are controlled by abusive relationships, addiction of alcohol or drugs, or enslavement to something else. Jesus has the anointing to permanently release these individuals and set them free.

#4: To give recovering of sight to the blind.

The fourth act of restoration Jesus offers is *recovery of sight to the blind*. This phrase "recovery of sight" is a translation of the Greek word *anablepsis*, which describes *the returning of one's sight, the restoration of sight*, or *to see again*. The word "blind" here is also important. It is the Greek word *tuphlos*, which means *blind*, but it doesn't just denote a person who is unable to see. It depicts *a person who has been intentionally blinded by someone else*. It can picture *one whose eyes have been deliberately removed so that he is blinded*. Thus, this individual hasn't just lost his sight: *he has no eyes with which to see*.

There are many people who have become blinded in life, and Jesus wants to come and restore their sight. Second Corinthians 4:4 says that Satan, "…the god of this world hath blinded the minds of them which believe not.…" This means the lost don't have spiritual eyes to see and understand the Gospel. Jesus has a specific anointing to create spiritual eyes in those who are spiritually blind, so that they can begin to see and hear and understand the truth. It is this same type of anointing that Jesus imparts to evangelists who carry the Good News to those who are lost and bound by sin.

#5: To set at liberty them that are bruised.

The fifth restorative work Jesus provides is an anointing *to set at liberty them that are bruised.* The phrase "set at liberty" is once again the Greek word *aphesis,* and while it describes *a release* or *a dismissal,* in this case, *it indicates a permanent release from the detrimental effects of a shattered life.* Specifically, the Greek here speaks of *a permanent release from the destructive effects of brokenness.*

Here is where the word "bruised" comes in. In Greek, it is the word *tethrausmenous,* and it means *to crush* or *to break down.* It depicts *a person who has been shattered or fractured by life; those whose lives have been continually split up and fragmented.* This would include husbands and wives — as well as their children — whose lives have been shattered by divorce. It is the exact Greek term from where we get the word *trauma.* Thus, Jesus came to set at liberty — *to give a permanent release* — to people who have been traumatized by life.

#6: To preach the acceptable year of the Lord.

In Luke 4:19, Jesus announced one more reason for the anointing of God on His life, and it was "to preach the acceptable year of the Lord." The word "acceptable" here is the Greek word *dektos,* and it means *favorable* or *accepted.* It describes *a favorable time or season to receive.* This means when the Lord comes on the scene, it is a divine moment and a favorable time to receive freedom, healing, and restoration for the poor, broken, blind, and anyone that has been traumatized by life.

Friend, Jesus is in the restoration business, and He wants to restore you in every area of your life where you've been blinded by hardships or become shattered by difficulties and disappointments. If you feel your life has fallen into ruins or become dismal and depressing, invite Jesus to begin working in those broken areas. Through the power of His Holy Spirit, He is able to restore you in ways that are exceeding and abundantly above and beyond all that you could ask or imagine! (*See* Ephesians 3:20.)

STUDY QUESTIONS

Study to shew thyself approved unto God, a workman that
needeth not to be ashamed, rightly dividing the word of truth.
— 2 Timothy 2:15

1. Luke 4:16 says that going to the synagogue was Jesus' "custom," which means going to church was His *habit*. How much of a priority has going to church and being an active part of a local group of believers been to you? What blessings come with being in God's house and with His people that you can't receive anywhere else? (Consider Hebrews 10:24,25; Micah 4:2; Psalm 84:4; Proverbs 27:17.)

2. Of the six kinds of restoration Jesus was anointed to do, which ones have you experienced personally and been blessed by? Which one (ones) would you really like to experience and/or see a loved one experience?

3. How does God respond to you when your heart is broken (contrite)? Consider Psalm 34:18 and 51:17; Isaiah 57:15 and 66:2.

PRACTICAL APPLICATION

But be ye doers of the word, and not hearers only,
deceiving your own selves.
— James 1:22

1. When a person is anointed to teach, sing, administrate, or serve in any way, it's usually visibly evident that God's hands are all over their life and work. What's at least one way God has touched and gifted *you* to be a blessing to others? Have any of the six restorative works of Jesus flowed through you? How has God worked through you to help transform others' lives?

2. When the Bible says Jesus was anointed to "heal," it uses the Greek word *iaomai*, which describes a healing that happens *progressively*, not instantaneously. What's one wound — physical, mental, emotional, or spiritual — that He's healed progressively in you?

3. Jesus says He is anointed to heal the "brokenhearted," which means He has the power and desire to progressively restore *people who have been walked on and crushed by others, or who feel they have been smashed to pieces by life or relationships.* How has life broken you? What have others done — or not done — that crushed you? Take a few minutes to talk through your feelings with God and invite Him to bring to completion the healing work that He wants to do in your heart.

TOPIC

Jesus Can Restore the Years You Have Lost

SCRIPTURES

1. **Joel 2:25,26** — And I will restore to you the years that the locust hath eaten, the cankerworm, and the caterpillar, and the palmerworm.... And ye shall eat in plenty, and be satisfied, and praise the name of the Lord your God, that hath dealt wondrously with you: and my people shall never be ashamed.

2. **Ephesians 5:16** — Redeeming the time, because the days are evil.

3. **Colossians 4:5** — Walk in wisdom toward them that are without, redeeming the time.

4. **Luke 19:10** — For the Son of man is come to seek and to save that which was lost.

GREEK WORDS

1. "lost" — ἀπολωλός (*apololos*): derived from the word *apollumi*, and it conveys the idea of something ruined, wasted, trashed, devastated, or destroyed; the same word for the Destroyer — one of the New Testament names to describe Satan's demented nature

2. "seek" — ζητέω (*zeteo*): to desire, to pursue, seek, or earnestly search for; a person so intent on achieving his goal that he will search, seek, and investigate, never giving up in his pursuit to get what he wants

3. "save" — σῴζω (*sodzo*): implies rescue, such as a rescue from a raging sea, rescue from an illness, rescue from immediate danger; inherent in this type of "rescue" is one's return to safety and soundness

SYNOPSIS

From 1766 to 1781, the Gatchina Palace was constructed under the order of Catherine the Great and stayed in the Romanov family for many generations. As we have seen, the Nazis invaded this breathtaking fortress in WWII, bombing and burning it, leaving it in a state of dreadful devastation. When restorers came in the mid-1970s, they chose to leave one room and only renovate a sliver of it, leaving the remainder of the room in its war-ravaged condition. The purpose was to provide visitors a vivid illustration of what the enemy had done and also show the remarkable effects of restoration.

As believers, we too have an enemy that is out to steal, kill, and destroy. But Jesus came that we might experience life in full abundance (*see* John 10:10). Are there parts of your life that have been negatively impacted by the work of the devil? What particular "room" has he ransacked and ravaged? These are the areas Jesus — the Great Restorer — wants to enter and completely put back together again! If your life is in need of any repairs, then *you are God's restoration project.*

The emphasis of this lesson:

Satan's attacks often come in waves, bringing great loss and devastation in our lives. But just as God promised to pay back Israel after they had suffered an invasion of pestilence, He promises to reimburse us for all that we have lost. Through Jesus, a full-scale rescue mission has been launched to restore what Satan has tried to steal, kill, and destroy.

A Brief Review of Our Previous Lessons

If we're honest, all of us would admit that we need some degree of restoration in one or more parts of our life. As we learned in Lesson 1, Satan is a kleptomaniac, always looking to steal something we have. If he can't steal it, he'll try to convince us it is beyond repair and that we should sacrifice it and move on. Ultimately, his goal is to totally obliterate our lives. In fact, we discovered in Lesson 2 that from the moment we came into this world, we were under Satan's control, being mindlessly manipulated by the changing whims of society.

When God saw our deplorable condition, He was moved by His great mercy and love to save us. Thus, He raised us up and gave us a brand new life in Christ Jesus (*see* Ephesians 2:1-5). We have become His "workmanship" — His *masterpiece* — having a life story with a wonderful new ending. Indeed, the Lord is our Good Shepherd who restores our soul (*see* Psalm 23:1-3), which is what we saw in Lesson 3.

And in Lesson 4, we unpacked the powerful meaning of Luke 4:16-19, which reveals six specific ways Jesus brings restoration in to our lives. He said, "The Spirit of the Lord is upon me, because he hath anointed me *to preach the gospel to the poor;* he hath sent me to *heal the brokenhearted, to preach deliverance to the captives,* and *recovering of sight to the blind, to set at liberty them that are bruised, to preach the acceptable year of the Lord."* (Luke 4:18,19).

Israel Had Suffered Loss
After Several Waves of Attack

There is a powerful promise of restoration God makes to us in Joel 2:25. He says, "And I will restore to you the years that the locust hath eaten, the cankerworm, and the caterpillar, and the palmerworm...." When God says, "I will restore," He is literally saying, *"I will make up to you,"* or *"I will compensate you."* He made this promise to the nation of Israel after they had experienced several years of successive attacks from locusts, cankerworms, caterpillars, and palmerworms.

What is interesting is that all four of these insects are manifestations of the same pestilence, each appearing in different phases. In the same way, when the enemy comes against us, it is often in phases — one wave of attack after another wave of attack after another. It appears that the locust, the cankerworm, the caterpillar, and the palmerworm had devoured virtually everything.

The Locust

Locusts are short-horned grasshoppers that are primarily found in places like Africa and Asia. As they migrate and grow, they change color, grow larger muscles, and gather into massive clouds that roll across landscapes and devastate crops. An individual locust can travel over 90 miles in a day, consuming its own weight as it travels. Can you imagine how much a swarm of locusts could consume as it makes its way across the land?

The Cankerworm

Cankerworms are the larvae (young grubs or caterpillars) that bring great destruction to fruit and shade trees, devouring both leaves and fruit. In Hebrew, the word "cankerworm" means *"the licking locust"* because they lick up the grass of the field as they move over it until nothing is left. When the Bible talks about cankerworms, it is likely referring to the locust at a certain stage of its growth, just as it emerges from the caterpillar state.

The Caterpillar

Caterpillars are also a devouring hoard. Like the cankerworm, they too are larvae (or wormlike young) but with a hairy exterior. They consume leaves, flowers, and plants and are mentioned in various places in Scripture, including Joel 2:25; Psalm 105:34; and Jeremiah 51:14.

The Palmerworm

Palmerworms are essentially hairy caterpillars that seem to suddenly appear on the leaves of plants and trees. The name "palmer" means *pilgrim*; hence, palmerworms wander or travel like pilgrims in large bands or swarms and devour everything in their path.

According to Joel 2:25, the locust, the cankerworm, the caterpillar, and the palmerworm had all come through in four consecutive years. With each successive wave of attack, God's people suffered the complete loss of their harvest. Yet, even though these swarms of pestilences marched like an insect army through the fields, destroying the crops and multiplying their number as they went, God promised to restore everything they had taken. That's the same promise God makes to you.

Have You Experienced Lost Years?

The "lost years" of our life are years that seem fruitless. During the years when the locusts had invaded the land and had eaten all the harvest, the Israelites had done a great deal of hard work. After everything was destroyed, the people must have thought, *All this work and what do I have to show for it?*

For you, your lost years may be a failed business venture, a bad investment, or an unsuccessful season in school. Maybe you put forth a lot of effort day-by-day, month-by-month, year-by-year to build a relationship only to see it fizzle out in disappointment. No one is immune to these types of experiences.

Lost years are painful years. Maybe you've lost a loved one. You had hopes and dreams for the future, but now you're alone and feel empty inside. The greater the love one has for another, the greater the grief. The pain of such a loss is often indescribable.

Lost years are often selfish years. Maybe you wasted time or made foolish decisions by not doing or living right. When you look back on those years, you have regrets that you didn't invest in important relationships because your priorities were out of line.

Lost years are loveless years. Oftentimes the enemy drives a wedge of offense between us and our spouse, our children, or a cherished friend. When we hold on to the offense and choose not to forgive, bitterness develops and our love grows cold. If you've been alienated from people you love, the void that results can weigh heavy on you.

Lost years are embarrassing years. When your relationships hit the rocks or you're blinded by selfishness and pride or you've made poor decisions with your finances, it can be extremely embarrassing. This can often lead to feelings of humiliation, condemnation, and even shame.

Nevertheless, in all these situations, Jesus is well-able to bring about restoration! He is in the restoration business, and He will restore to you the lost years of your life. His promise to the people of Israel is also His promise to you: "And ye shall eat in plenty, and be satisfied, and praise the name of the Lord your God, that hath dealt wondrously with you: and my people shall never be ashamed" (Joel 2:26).

Have you lost money? It can be restored. How about property or relationships? They can be restored too. Even time can be restored. In Ephesians 5:16, God talks about "Redeeming the time, because the days are evil." The word "redeeming" means *to buy it back* or *get it back again*. This same instruction is repeated in Colossians 4:5, which tells us, "Walk in wisdom toward them that are without, redeeming the time." Again, the word "redeeming" means *to buy something back* or *get something back that you thought was lost*.

If you have lost precious time with those you love or missed opportunities, humble yourself and pray, asking God for His grace to buy back the time you lost (*see* 2 Corinthians 9:8; James 4:6). His grace is truly amazing and can enable you to do what you could never do on your own.

God Is Able To Restore What Was Lost

God begins the process of restoring your lost years as you draw closer to Him in relationship. The people of Israel in Joel's time had endured much loss, but as they turned to seek God and deepen their relationship with Him, He responded by saying, "…You shall know that I am in the midst of Israel, and that I am the Lord your God and there is no other.

My people shall never be put to shame" (Joel 2:27 *NKJV*). God drew close to His people in communion, and they experienced far greater fellowship than anything they had ever known before.

The Bible says, "Draw near to God and He will draw near to you…" (James 4:8 *NKJV*). When you humble yourself and reach out to God for help, that humility attracts Him like metal to a magnet. He draws near to you, bringing with Him every good and perfect gift you can imagine (*see* James 1:17). This includes all the restorative works of Jesus we learned about in Luke 4:16-19 (For a more detailed review of these, *see* Lesson 4).

God can also restore your lost years by multiplying your fruitfulness. The harvests for the nation of Israel during Joel's day had been wiped out for four years, but God restored the years that the locusts had eaten by giving them bumper harvests. Remember, God is no respecter of persons (*see* Acts 10:34). What He did for Israel then He can certainly do for you now. If you've suffered loss, humble yourself before the Lord and ask Him to get involved and honor His promise to restore what has been lost in your life.

Jesus Is on a Rescue Mission, Seeking To Save What Has Been Lost

As we wrap up our study, let's look once more at Jesus' primary mission recorded in Luke 19:10, which says, "For the Son of man is come to seek and to save that which was lost." Now you may have heard this verse and been told that Jesus is talking about evangelism here. Although it is true that He came to bring salvation to those who are lost, that is not the only thing He is telling us in this verse. The broader meaning here is that Jesus has come to restore everything that has been lost.

The word **"lost"** in this verse is the Greek word *apololos*, which is derived from the word *apollumi*. It conveys the idea of something *ruined, wasted, trashed, devastated,* or *destroyed.* It is the same word used in the New Testament for the *Destroyer* — one of the names that describes Satan's demented nature. The word *apollumi* comes from the word *luo*, which is used in Luke 3:16. In this verse, John the Baptist talks about Jesus and says, "…One mightier than I cometh, the latchet of whose shoes I am not worthy to unloose…." The word "unloose" is the word *luo*, which means *to untie* or *to unravel something until it completely comes undone.*

The use of this word tells us that when the devil does his destructive work, he tries to unravel any area of our life he can until we feel like we are coming apart at the seams. Thus, Jesus came to seek and to save that which is *falling to pieces and coming undone*. If there are areas in your life that seem to be falling apart, pray and give them to Jesus. Putting things back together is His specialty.

Luke 19:10 says Jesus is *seeking* after people whose lives seem to be in pieces. The word **"seek"** here is the Greek word *zeteo*, which means *to desire, to pursue, to seek*, or *earnestly search for*. It is a picture of a person so intent on achieving his goal that he will search, seek, and investigate, never giving up in his pursuit to get what he wants. That is what Jesus is doing. He is fiercely seeking and searching for lost people and the things people have lost. Why? So He can *save* them.

In Greek, the word **"save"** is *sodzo*, which implies *rescue*, such as *a rescue from a raging sea, a rescue from an illness*, or *a rescue from immediate danger*. Inherent in this type of "rescue" is one's return to safety and soundness, which tells us Jesus' work to save us isn't just a *salvage operation* — it's a *full-scale rescue* that results in a *fully restorative operation*. To be clear: When Christ finishes His work in us, we are *not* a weaker, substandard version of what we used to be. We are stronger and better because of what Jesus has done to *restore* our lives.

Friend, you can know without a doubt that Jesus *has put forth* and *is putting forth* His best efforts to actively seek, save, and restore whatever Satan has tried to steal, kill, or destroy. He is seeking to perform a rescue operation in every area of *your* life where devastation and ruin exist. He also seeks to rescue and restore those around you who need it. So don't give up on yourself or others because rescue operations really are Jesus' specialty!

STUDY QUESTIONS

Study to shew thyself approved unto God, a workman that needeth not to be ashamed, rightly dividing the word of truth.
— 2 Timothy 2:15

1. What did David say about how God restores our lives in Psalm 103:3-6,8-18?

2. What can we learn from Paul's response to his "lost years"? (*See* Philippians 3:13,14.)

3. According to Hebrews 4:15 and 16, what does God want you to do when you're hurting or in trouble? What does Hebrews 2:17 and 18 say is the reason Jesus is able to understand and help you with what you're going through? How do these passages give you new hope for your future?

PRACTICAL APPLICATION

**But be ye doers of the word, and not hearers only,
deceiving your own selves.
— James 1:22**

1. When you look back over your life, are there times you would consider "lost"? Are there days, months, or years when you exerted a great deal of effort and energy, but you were left with nothing to show for it? Briefly describe what took place.

2. How does it encourage you to know that God not only *can* but also *wants* to restore what has been lost in your life?

3. By now, you've probably come to the realization that *you* can't fix yourself or restore what has been lost or stolen from your life. Instead, the only way to experience the restoration God wants for you is to humbly ask Him to do what only He can do for you. Take time now to stop and pray: *Father, thank You for wanting to restore my life fully and completely. I invite You to come in and begin working to reverse the devastation the enemy has caused. Restore Your peace, joy, and love in my life and in my family. Heal the wounds from harsh words people have spoken and restore the broken places in my soul. Help me understand and live the abundant life Jesus died to give me. I love You, Father! In Jesus name. Amen*

Notes

CLAIM YOUR FREE RESOURCE!

As a way of introducing you further to the teaching ministry of Rick Renner, we would like to send you free of charge his teaching CD, "How To Receive a Miraculous Touch From God."

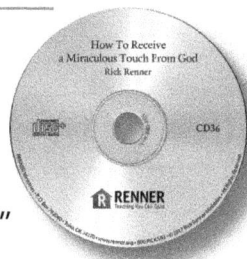

In His earthly ministry, Jesus commonly healed *all* who were sick of *all* their diseases. In this profound message, learn about the manifold dimensions of Christ's wisdom, goodness, power, and love toward all humanity who came to Him in faith with their needs.

☑ **YES, I want to receive Rick Renner's monthly teaching letter!**

Simply scan the QR code to claim this resource or go to:
renner.org/claim-your-free-offer